START YOUR NETWORK MARKETING BUSINESS

ARVIND UPADHYAY

Copyright © Arvind Upadhyay
All Rights Reserved.

ISBN 978-1-68563-250-2

This book has been published with all efforts taken to make the material error-free after the consent of the author. However, the author and the publisher do not assume and hereby disclaim any liability to any party for any loss, damage, or disruption caused by errors or omissions, whether such errors or omissions result from negligence, accident, or any other cause.

While every effort has been made to avoid any mistake or omission, this publication is being sold on the condition and understanding that neither the author nor the publishers or printers would be liable in any manner to any person by reason of any mistake or omission in this publication or for any action taken or omitted to be taken or advice rendered or accepted on the basis of this work. For any defect in printing or binding the publishers will be liable only to replace the defective copy by another copy of this work then available.

One of the things I love so much about network marketing is the people. As you listen to this training, pretend we're sitting in your kitchen — or your living room, or your office — and we're having a conversation about starting your network marketing business. Or maybe you're restarting your network marketing business. Maybe you started once before, stumbled a little bit, and need to restart. It's OK. I want to help you build new muscles in this profession. In this program, I'm going to share with you everything I wish someone had shared with me when I first got started in network marketing. If you start right, you can save yourself so much challenge, anguish, and grief. You don't need to suffer through the school of hard knocks. I'd like to save you from that pain. That's the purpose of this course. I want you to believe in yourself. The vehicle is there. All you have to do is get in and drive. I want to personally walk through the process with you. This is less of a "how-to" training program and more of a conversation on how we can work together to help you achieve your goals in Network Marketing, and do it fast. "An early-morning walk is a blessing for the whole day." – Henry David Thoreau The simple act of walking can be a tremendous boost to your focus, productivity, clarity of mind, not to mention your health and waistline. Recently a fellow blogger wrote to me talking about how many pounds she lost on vacation because she walked all day long — something many of us have experienced. She ended by saying, "If only I could find the time to walk 6 hours a day." That got me to ask — why not? Why can't we work out a routine where we walk all day long? What follows are a couple of radical but incredibly fulfilling and productive changes from most people's daily routine. I think they're worthy of consideration if you: » have any control over your schedule; » can work from different locations; » want to get more active and trim your waistline; and » need to find new ways to focus and get important things done. I recently tried both these routines and loved them, and am working them into my life in different ways. 103 1. The Walking Vacation Working Routine I love going on vacation, not only for the food and sights and history and culture and people, but for the walking. You get in amazing shape by walking around all day, exploring, taking frequent breaks but staying on your feet for at least half the day. Why should we reserve this fantastic routine to vacations? Just because we need to get work done? Consider a routine that consists of alternating short walks with work: 1.

Walk for 20-30 minutes to a location: coffee shop, library, park, beach, cafe or bistro, peaceful rest spot, etc. Don't use mobile devices as you walk – remain disconnected. 2. Work or read for 30-40 minutes: write, take notes, read, respond to emails, design, meet with a colleague or client, make calls, whatever. You can also have coffee, some water, fruits, a small meal, and so on. 3. Repeat as many times as you can. This is a bit of a nomadic work schedule, roaming from one place to another, but it has numerous benefits: 1. When you walk, you can think, which is something that's hard to do when you're sitting and distracted all day. When you get to your destination, write down all the notes from your walking contemplation. 2. When you walk, you can also clear your head, meditate, or just enjoy your surroundings and relieve stress. 3. You get into tremendous shape by walking so much. 4. Your work will also be more focused, because you have less time to work. Use the 30-40 minute bursts of work for important tasks that you think about as you walk. 104 5. Some stops can be in spots without a wireless connection, which means you'll get more work done without the distraction of the Internet. 2. The Disconnect and Connect Working Routine A number of people have announced vacations from the Internet, when they go a few days or a week or even a month without any connection — on purpose. This serves as a way for them to reconnect with life, to find focus and get important things done, and to enjoy the peace of disconnection. But why make it an occasional "cleanse"? Why not build it into your routine? Consider a routine such as the following: 1. Disconnect for a day (or two). No Internet connection — perhaps no computer at all if using your computer is too much of a temptation to connect. Use an actual paper notepad and pen, writing and brainstorming and making pages of notes or sketches. Make phone calls instead of connecting via email or IM. Meet with people in real life, and get outside. Get a ton of important work done. No mobile devices except for actual phone calls. 2. Then connect for a day (or two). Take all the notes and work you did during your disconnect, and type them up and email them and post them online and so forth. Answer emails and get other routine tasks done, and then prepare for your next day of disconnect. 3. Repeat. You can vary the number of days you're disconnected or connected, finding the balance that works for you. While some may feel this will limit the work they can do, I think it'll actually do the opposite: you'll get more done, or at least more important tasks done, because you won't be distracted. 105 You'll also find it a calming change from the always-connected. It's a peaceful routine. Conclusions The purpose of these two routines isn't to tell you how to work, because we must each find the style and routine that works for our particular job. It's to show you that change is possible, and that if you think outside the usual, you can find some exciting possibilities. You don't need to do these things exactly the way I've outlined above, but you can find a blend that works best for you. Perhaps a hybrid routine that uses both concepts, or a once-a-week walking or disconnect period. Integrating walking into your work routine can do wonders for your fitness and for your focus. That's something you can't find if you're sitting all day. Integrating disconnection into your work routine will allow you to get even more done, and to find peace of mind. I urge you to consider both, and see how they can make your life better.

Contents

Foreword — ix

Preface — xv

Acknowledgements — xxi

1. Introduction — 1
2. Types Of Network Marketing Businesses — 2
3. How To Find The Right Network Marketing Business — 4
4. Network Marketing Strategy That Works — 12
5. Start Your Network Marketing Business — 19
6. 11 Tips To Help You Network Better! — 26

Networking Is The Exchange Of Information — 39

Foreword

Network marketing or Multi-level Network Marketing (MLM) is a method of marketing that makes use of independent sales reps as a way to reach a wider range of networks, where conventional methods such as traditional online or offline advertising wouldn't work. It is a very popular business opportunity for people looking to work part-time doing flexible jobs. Hundreds of companies utilize this method, including some well-known brands such as Avon, Tupperware and Mary Kay Cosmetics: these companies and their respective associates hire a 'sales force', much like insurance companies have been doing for years, and they use these individuals to reach networks such as friends and family. Ever come across an ad on TV using the term "Independent Insurance Agent", or something similar? These individuals are not really employees of the company; they operate independently by purchasing a product sample starter kit, which usually costs a few hundred dollars, and with that they get an opportunity to sell the product line to their own contacts, friends, family, etc. These types of programs rely on an individual's ability to influence their network and sell products; and when properly executed, both parties benefit. Many network marketing programs require participants to recruit more sales reps, and as a participant adds to their own "downline", sales made by the new recruits generates income for those above them. 4 Compensation cannot be made exclusively on the basis of recruitment: instead, it should be based on the ability to sell company services and/or products. If a network marketing program generates revenue almost entirely from these recruitments then it may be illegal, and by definition would be a pyramid scheme. A network marketing program is usually exempt from traditional business regulation and state and federal laws don't define it as franchises under franchise law, so you may need to do some research before putting in any money.

. What do you want out of your network marketing career? Most people who begin in network marketing want to get their investment back, have some success, make some profit, and see what happens. As you get started, your reasons will drive everything. Your reasons will push you through the pain. They will cause you to act, maybe even to face your fears. Strong reasons are strong drivers. Weak reasons sometimes aren't enough to drive you to success. Get a clear picture in your mind. Why are you doing this? If money was not an object, what would you want to do with your life? Maybe you want a nicer house, nicer car, or a better school for your kids. What is it?

2. What are you willing to give up to get it? Time Think about how much time you can carve out of your current day to build your future in network marketing. How much time can you invest? If your reasons are strong, you'll figure out the time. Do you spend a lot of time on sports or other recreation that you can put aside, and focus on what you need to do to get your business started right? Money It will also cost you some money to get started. You will need to invest some money into your business. You will need to buy some books, attend some trainings, travel to events in order to learn necessary skills. You might need to put some hobbies on hold while you create a new income stream. Habits A lot of people have habits that they can change. Many people put in the minimum effort at work and then come home and turn off completely. Or they use all of their leisure time to hang out with friends and waste hours, days, weeks. Others procrastinate, blame others, or sit back and wait for someone to tell them what to do instead of taking initiative. Exercise: How much time can you carve out of each day to build your future? How much money are you willing to invest in to your business to build it right? What do you need to give up or put aside while you do this?

"An early-morning walk is a blessing for the whole day." – Henry David Thoreau The simple act of walking can be a tremendous boost to your focus, productivity, clarity of mind, not to mention your health and waistline. Recently a fellow blogger wrote to me talking about how many pounds she lost on vacation because she walked all day long — something many of us have experienced. She ended by saying, "If only I could find the time to walk 6 hours a day." That got me to ask — why not? Why can't we work out a routine where we walk all day long? What follows are a couple of radical but incredibly fulfilling and productive changes from most people's daily routine. I think they're worthy of consideration if you: » have any control over your schedule; » can work from different locations; » want to get more active and trim your waistline; and » need to find new ways to focus and get important things done. I recently tried both these routines and loved them, and am working them into my life in different ways. 103 1. The Walking Vacation Working Routine I love going on vacation, not only for the food and sights and history and culture and people, but for the walking. You get in amazing shape by walking around all day, exploring, taking frequent breaks but staying on your feet for at least half the day. Why should we reserve this fantastic routine to vacations? Just because we need to get work done? Consider a routine that consists of alternating short walks with work: 1. Walk for 20-30 minutes to a location: coffee shop, library, park, beach, cafe or bistro, peaceful rest spot, etc. Don't use mobile devices as you walk – remain disconnected. 2. Work or read for 30-40 minutes: write, take notes, read, respond to emails, design, meet with a colleague or client, make calls, whatever. You can also have coffee, some water, fruits, a small meal, and so on. 3. Repeat as many times as you can. This is a bit of a nomadic work schedule, roaming from one place to another, but it has numerous benefits: 1. When you walk, you can think, which is something that's hard to do when you're sitting and distracted all day. When you get to your destination, write down all the notes from your walking contemplation. 2. When you walk, you can also clear your head, meditate, or just enjoy your surroundings and relieve stress. 3. You get into tremendous shape by walking so much. 4. Your work will also be more focused, because you have less time to work. Use the 30-40 minute bursts of work for important tasks that you think about as you walk. 104 5. Some stops can be in spots without a wireless connection, which means you'll get more work done without the distraction of the Internet. 2. The Disconnect and Connect Working Routine A number of people have announced vacations from the Internet, when they go a few days or a week or even a month without any connection — on purpose. This serves as a way for them to reconnect with life, to find focus and get important things done, and to enjoy the peace of disconnection. But why make it an occasional "cleanse"? Why not build it into your routine? Consider a routine such as the following: 1. Disconnect for a day (or two). No Internet connection — perhaps no computer at all if using your computer is too much of a temptation to connect. Use an actual paper notepad and pen, writing and brainstorming and making pages of notes or sketches. Make phone calls instead of connecting via email or IM. Meet with people in real life, and get outside. Get a ton of important work done. No mobile devices except for actual phone calls. 2. Then connect for a day (or two). Take all the notes and work you did during your disconnect, and type them up and email them and post them online and so forth. Answer emails and get other routine tasks done, and then prepare for your next day of disconnect. 3. Repeat. You can vary the number of days you're disconnected or connected, finding the balance that works for you. While some may feel this will limit the work they can do, I think it'll actually do the opposite: you'll get more done, or at least more important tasks done, because you won't be distracted. 105 You'll also find it a calming change from the always-connected. It's a peaceful routine. Conclusions The purpose of these two routines isn't to tell you how to work, because we must each find the style and routine that works for our particular job. It's to show you that change is possible, and that if you think outside the usual, you can find some exciting possibilities. You don't need to do these things exactly the way I've outlined above, but you can find a blend that works best for you. Perhaps a hybrid routine that uses both concepts, or a once-a-week walking or disconnect period. Integrating walking into your work routine can do wonders for your fitness and for your focus. That's something you can't find if you're sitting all day. Integrating disconnection into your work routine will allow you to get even more done, and to find peace of mind. I urge you to consider both, and see how they can make your life better.

"An early-morning walk is a blessing for the whole day." – Henry David Thoreau The simple act of walking can be a tremendous boost to your focus, productivity, clarity of mind, not to mention your health and waistline. Recently a fellow blogger wrote to me talking about how many pounds she lost on vacation because she walked all day long — something many of us have experienced. She ended by saying, "If only I could find the time to walk 6 hours a day." That got me to ask — why not? Why can't we work out a routine where we walk all day long? What follows are a couple of radical but incredibly fulfilling and productive changes from most people's daily routine. I think they're worthy of consideration if you: » have any control over your schedule; » can work from different locations; » want to get more active and trim your waistline; and » need to find new ways to focus and get important things done. I recently tried both these routines and loved them, and am working them into my life in different ways. 103 1. The Walking Vacation Working Routine I love going on vacation, not only for the food and sights and history and culture and people, but for the walking. You get in amazing shape by walking around all day, exploring, taking frequent breaks but staying on your feet for at least half the day. Why should we reserve this fantastic routine to vacations? Just because we need to get work done? Consider a routine that consists of alternating short walks with work: 1. Walk for 20-30 minutes to a location: coffee shop, library, park, beach, cafe or bistro, peaceful rest spot, etc. Don't use mobile devices as you walk – remain disconnected. 2. Work or read for 30-40 minutes: write, take notes, read, respond to emails, design, meet with a colleague or client, make calls, whatever. You can also have coffee, some water, fruits, a small meal, and so on. 3. Repeat as many times as you can. This is a bit of a nomadic work schedule, roaming from one place to another, but it has numerous benefits: 1. When you walk, you can think, which is something that's hard to do when you're sitting and distracted all day. When you get to your destination, write down all the notes from your walking contemplation. 2. When you walk, you can also clear your head, meditate, or just enjoy your surroundings and relieve stress. 3. You get into tremendous shape by walking so much. 4. Your work will also be more focused, because you have less time to work. Use the 30-40 minute bursts of work for important tasks that you think about as you walk. 104 5. Some stops can be in spots without a wireless connection, which means you'll get more work done without the distraction of the Internet. 2. The Disconnect and Connect Working Routine A number of people have announced vacations from the Internet, when they go a few days or a week or even a month without any connection — on purpose. This serves as a way for them to reconnect with life, to find focus and get important things done, and to enjoy the peace of disconnection. But why make it an occasional "cleanse"? Why not build it into your routine? Consider a routine such as the following: 1. Disconnect for a day (or two). No Internet connection — perhaps no computer at all if using your computer is too much of a temptation to connect. Use an actual paper notepad and pen, writing and brainstorming and making pages of notes or sketches. Make phone calls instead of connecting via email or IM. Meet with people in real life, and get outside. Get a ton of important work done. No mobile devices except for actual phone calls. 2. Then connect for a day (or two). Take all the notes and work you did during your disconnect, and type them up and email them and post them online and so forth. Answer emails and get other routine tasks done, and then prepare for your next day of disconnect. 3. Repeat. You can vary the number of days you're disconnected or connected, finding the balance that works for you. While some may feel this will limit the work they can do, I think it'll actually do the opposite: you'll get more done, or at least more important tasks done, because you won't be distracted. 105 You'll also find it a calming change from the always-connected. It's a peaceful routine. Conclusions The purpose of these two routines isn't to tell you how to work, because we must each find the style and routine that works for our particular job. It's to show you that change is possible, and that if you think outside the usual, you can find some exciting possibilities. You don't need to do these things exactly the way I've outlined above, but you can find a blend that works best for you. Perhaps a hybrid routine that uses both concepts, or a once-a-week walking or disconnect period. Integrating walking into your work routine can do wonders for your fitness and for your network business.

Preface

What are the secrets to building an ultra-successful network marketing business? If you were to ask 30 top distributors and industry leaders, you'd get 30 different answers with many areas of commonality. Each would also possess some totally unique insights into what it
takes derived from their own field experiences that would not necessarily be shared by the others.

For more than 50 years, throughout the great profession of network marketing, the gift of a life-changing income, the opportunity to take part in fun and fulfilling work, and the chance to forever impact the lives of countless others has been shared by many top leaders and expert trainers in their own ways. Each of these extraordinary individuals has been successful in conveying the essential principles that have allowed their students (downline) to go out and touch the lives of countless others, creating wealth and with it, personal freedom in the process.

All of these experts, in building their personal fortunes through the vehicle of network marketing, have developed their own insights into what this process requires. And each has acquired some very special success distinctions that have supported their teams to duplicate their achievements to some degree. That is the very special gift that network marketing embodies: Those who reach top levels of accomplishment must have done so by supporting several others to duplicate their success and build networking dynasties of their own. No other profession better rewards its members for the exact levels of success they are able to convey to others. Networkers truly earn what they are worth!

Clearly, each of these networking gurus has much to share, as is evident by the wealth they have championed others to create and the lives they have forever influenced by sharing the awesome gift that networking can be. Many of these experts have written books, recorded tapes, conducted trainings, or otherwise shared their wisdom with others who have benefited from it. So, we asked ourselves the question: How powerful would it be if we could persuade each of these experts to share that one area of expertise they feel most significantly contributed to their own success and to that of their organizations and students? What if we could compile this cumulative wisdom in one book? What if we could share with others those special breakthroughs and closely guarded secrets that resulted in each of these gurus experiencing top-shelf accomplishment levels? Would we not then be able to create a synergistic effect, whereby 2 + 2 does not equal simply 4 but perhaps 40 or even 400?

And that's exactly what we did. As a leading network marketing distributor and trainer, I handpicked those I consider to be the best of the best, the most knowledgeable experts in the network marketing profession. I interviewed hundreds of top distributors, authors, and trainers. From this elite group, I selected these 36 distributors, trainers, and industry leaders and invited them to submit a chapter apiece containing the special wisdom they believe to be responsible for creating their own successful dynasties and those of their students. These leaders were instructed to share actual secrets and tips that they knew would support people to be successful if they utilized this knowledge. No untested or speculative theories, just proven pearls that would have a significant impact on the business-building potential of the book's readers.

The resultant topics you are soon to read about span every aspect necessary to build an ultra-successful network marketing business. They include such critical areas as visioning, prospecting, enrolling, training, building belief, creating personal development structures necessary for top success, and many more. Secrets in the realm of leadership development will be shared, as well as a wide variety of business-building techniques and pathways, from traditional to online building systems, from trade shows to direct mail to party plans. You'll read about the actual tools that these experts shared with their organizations, making them successful in the process. All the key success principles and other areas of focus necessary to build a top network marketing business will be revealed.

The result of this compilation of wisdom from these trainers represents hundreds, perhaps thousands of hours of private training sessions, many to this point shared only within their own companies and personal organizations. The sheer magnitude of the ideas led to this book's title: The Ultimate Guide to Network Marketing.

With a few notable exceptions, most network marketing books available today are anecdotal by nature. They share stories of individuals who have achieved success in the network marketing industry. These stories, while interesting and valuable, are no substitution for actual insights into how to build a top organization. To my knowledge, this is the first network marketing book written that gives readers a variety of different informed perspectives around what is necessary to achieve top success. It offers readers a wide variety of proven business-building techniques from many of the most successful network marketing leaders in the industry. It also offers the perspective of a great cross section of well-known top distributors and industry leaders who share the secrets they attribute to creating their own success.

To follow are 37 chapters outlining the core competencies necessary to build wealth while elucidating the leadership concepts that are of critical importance to building an ultimately successful organization.

In Chapter 1, Brian Biro shares how we can all create daily windows of opportunity to transform our lives and businesses. From deciding to live and work from a state of constant gratitude to paying attention to where you focus moment by moment, Biro supports us to pay keen attention to managing our thoughts if we want our businesses to grow and prosper. John Terhune, CEO of Rainmaker Consulting, expands upon this concept as he shares how top success always begins with the proper attitude. He gives step-by-step instructions about how to craft your winning attitude necessary to attract others to you like a magnet. Master motivational speaker Jim Rohn continues on this theme by discussing the qualities he sees as essential to any networker's success. He shares how anyone can start a business with no capital as long as the entrepreneur possesses these critical components.

Cliff Walker, top distributor and industry trainer from England, shares the nine key tasks that make up his winning strategies for duplicating network marketing achievement. See how well you measure up in each of these nine areas by taking Cliff's quiz to clarify where you stand. Shore up any lacking areas, and your business will be back on track. Mark Stevens, CEO of a very successful network marketing company, talks about the power of a great system and why the system is the key factor that can keep distributors on the right track headed toward fulfillment of their dreams. He outlines all the essential components of the system he teaches to his own company's distributors.

Dave Klaybor has been both the CEO of a successful network marketing company and a top distributor. He discusses how our behaviors are shaped by our thoughts and other critical factors. When we are able to recognize what's missing in this critical cycle, we can put it into place to ensure that our behavior will result in the accomplishment of the objects we desire. Glenn and Marian Head of an industry leading magazine, Networking Times, outline what the vital signs of a healthy business are. Put your life and business to the test and see how you measure up.

Of course, if you ask any successful networkers, most will tell you that a rock-solid belief level must form the foundation for all accomplishment. Master motivator Steve Siebold discusses the importance of mental toughness. He tells us how we can master our emotions to create a productive business. Art Burleigh tells us why belief is so vital to our businesses and how to build it so that you are unshakable. Top distributor Dan Conlon lists the stages successful entrepreneurs must master if they are to build a business methodically. Learn what the essential components of each stage are and put any missing elements into place for your business.

undergraduates, addresses the challenges of teaching and learning when prerequisite knowledge varies greatly from student to student. The authors had three main goals when writing this text: 1. To write a text that students can easily comprehend 2. To make connections between what students are learning and how they may apply that knowledge 3. To give flexibility to instructors to tailor a course to the needs of their students. Many elements play a role in determining a book's effectiveness for students. Not only is it critical that the text be accurate and readable, but also, in order for a book to be effective, aspects such as the page design, the interactive nature of the presentation, and the ability to support and challenge all students have an incredible impact on how easily students comprehend the material. Here are some of the ways this text addresses the needs of students at all levels: ■■ Page layout is clean and free of potentially distracting elements. ■■ Matched Problems that accompany each of the completely worked examples help students gain solid knowledge of the basic topics and assess their own level of understanding before moving on. ■■ Review material (Appendix A and Chapter 1) can be used judiciously to help remedy gaps in prerequisite knowledge. ■■ A Diagnostic Prerequisite Test prior to Chapter 1 helps students assess their skills, while the Basic Algebra Review in Appendix A provides students with the content they need to remediate those skills. ■■ Explore and Discuss problems lead the discussion into new concepts or build upon a current topic. They help students of all levels gain better insight into the mathematical concepts through thought-provoking questions that are effective in both small and large classroom settings. ■■ Instructors are able to easily craft homework assignments that best meet the needs of their students by taking advantage of the variety of types and difficulty levels of the exercises. Exercise sets at the end of each section consist of a Skills Warm-up (four to eight problems that review prerequisite knowledge specific to that section) followed by problems divided into categories A, B, and C by level of difficulty, with level-C exercises being the most challenging.

Acknowledgements

I would like to thank to supervisor of notionpress for the valuable guidance and advice. He inspired usgreatly to work in this project. His willingness to motivate uscontributed tremendously to our project. I also would like tothank him for showing us some example that related to thetopic of our project. Besides, I would like to thank theauthority of Shri Ram College of Commerce for providing witha good environment and facilities to complete this project. Iwould like to express my gratitude towards my parents fortheir kind co-operation and encouragement which help me incompletion of this project.My thanks and appreciations also go to my colleague indeveloping the project and people who have willingly helpedmeout with their abilities.

ONE
INTRODUCTION

Multi-level marketingMLM is a marketing strategy in which the sales force is
compensated not only for sales they personally generate, but also for the sales ofthe othersalespeople thatthey recruit.This recruitedsales force isreferred to asthe participant's"downline", andcan providemultiple levels ofcompensation. Other terms usedfor MLMinclude pyramid
selling, networkmarketingCompanies that use MLM models for compensation have been a frequent subject ofcriticism and lawsuits. Criticism has focused on their similarity to illegal pyramid
schemes, cult-like behaviour, price fixing of products, high initial entry costs (for
marketing kit and first products), emphasis on recruitment of others over actualsales, encouraging if not requiring members to purchase and use the company'sproducts, exploitation of personal relationships as both sales and recruitingtargets, complex and sometimes exaggerated compensation schemes, the companymaking major money off its training events and materials, and cult-like techniqueswhich some groups use to enhance their members' enthusiasm and devotion.

TWO
Types of Network Marketing Businesses

Most network marketing companies operate as some form of multi-level marketing plan, where the company provides a product or service and assigns agents to sell it. This setup gives the sales reps an opportunity to earn a commission by selling products, and recruiting new reps and growing their own little network. Direct marketing works in a similar fashion, where a product line is launched to the market, and the company invests in a range of marketing materials including training and tools to help the new investors become successful. Commission largely depends on the number of items sold over a period of time and if there is an existing market to tap into, products can sell out in large volumes. Individuals seeking out a more family-friendly type of network marketing could try out party plans, which are popular with parents who want an additional revenue stream. Party plan systems require an initial investment to create websites, buy product demons and relevant marketing materials, but their flexible scheduling makes them ideal for anyone splitting their time between the company and other responsibilities. Technology allows sales representatives to expand existing networks and tap into new ones in order to establish a wider revenue stream. As their 7 down-line expands, so does the commission and with a big-enough downline your leg work reduces and you start earning from the new reps. But before you get to this point, you have to select the right type of system and have a plan of action. The different types of networks Here are the different structures available in network marketing:

1. Unilevel Structure This system allows you to earn from your frontline and it doesn't limit the number of people you can sign. It's a pretty old system and it's certainly not the most lucrative but it does promote cross-line competition, which means a higher chance of expansion. 2. Stair Step Breakaway Plan Perfect for the aggressive marketer, this plan is excellent if you have plenty of time to dedicate to sales. The higher you go up the steps, the more you break up from your own up-line, and in the end you'll only have people on your down-line, which means people will stop earning from you. If for instance you're supposed to breakaway at step 7, your up-line won't earn from you anymore, and you will get all commissions from anyone below you. 3. The Binary System 8 This system has been popularized by Questnet and it takes significant dedication to earn from. You only get two down-lines with this plan and new sign-ins are automatically under your down-line. In order to make money you have to earn from both down-lines; so when picking out this type of plan, try to get one where you can carry over extra points from the less active binary side. 4. Forced Matrix Plan This system aims to promote teamwork and it allows newcomers to earn high commissions by combining forces with fellow members. Because it has a defined frontline, the system allows members to focus on signing more people in order to earn on higher levels.

Types of Network Marketing Businesses

THREE

How To Find The Right Network Marketing Business

If you'd gotten into network marketing a few years ago, there were very few companies doing it and back then people didn't spend weeks trying to find the right type of marketing business. But that is not the case today and in order to achieve any kind of success you have to be with the right company. There are literally thousands of companies available and new ones are popping up every other week, so the job of choosing the right one won't be easy. One of the ways many people get into network marketing is because a friend or family member introduced them to a company but often this is not the best way because the company might not be suited for them. The result, often times, is frustration, failure or moderate success; all of which can be avoided. Working with the right company doesn't automatically guarantee success, but it certainly increases your chances of attaining it. Ultimately what makes a person successful in network marketing is what they do, and that means building a network of people keen on purchasing a product or using a service. It's simple enough; you only need to provide information about 10 the product or service, answer whatever questions your prospects might have, make the sale, do a little follow-up, sponsor them, train and support. Your passion for the job and desire for success will make all this simple and fun, and there's no way to get to that place if you don't believe in the company you work for. As a network marketer, you want to feel secure in the company, and for financial reasons you want to believe that it will be there for years to come, supporting you and your family. So how do you get around to choosing the right company for you? There are dozens of factors to consider but some people only need a few assurances before joining a company. We'll look at a number of issues just to make sure you are covered. 1. How long has the company been around for? In order to make sure the effort you put in today will pay off for many years to come, select a company that's proven to be durable. This shouldn't be too difficult to work out: majority of network marketing companies, about 90%, fail within the first two years. Nobody wants to invest their time and energy into a company that can't guarantee continuity, so start by looking at this and you will shorten the list of companies significantly. 2. Are they well capitalized? In simpler words, you're trying to find out if they have the cash needed to grow, bring in talented management, develop solid infrastructure, keep up 11 with technology, and of course, pay your commissions. One way to make sure no company gets past your radar is to focus on public traded companies for the sole reason that they are required to disclose their finances to the authorities. Some of this information might be harder to access when dealing with private companies, so keep that in mind. 3. Is there a need for the product or service? There are many horror stories about people who wasted their money purchasing products they don't really need. To avoid all the drama that comes with that, find out if whatever the company is selling fills a genuine void, if it actually helps people, and if it comes at a reasonable price. The product should provide value to the customer; otherwise the whole plan will fail. 4. Trend or fad? Some products hit the market and generate huge waves of customer appeal but only for a short time, until they fade out. You might be able to make a good amount of money while the excitement goes on but the problem is you can't create any long-term residual income on a product that lasts a couple of months before fading off into oblivion. Consider the long-term effect and find out if customers would be interested in using the product or service for a long time, that way your income won't run out. 5. Are you able to generate immediate income? 12 This would pay off if you're keen on expanding your network but the only way to ensure you get ready cash flow is to tap into an existing market. If you can locate a large untapped market for your product, that would be a good place to start. 6. Technology Not everyone has fun doing sales work, but anybody can appreciate working in an environment that involves plugging into a system and using a bunch of tools to do the sorting and selling for you. Technology can be used to narrow down the targets and make your work a whole lot easier. One advantage of having machines do the heavy-lifting is it allows you more time for yourself, and if you have another job to get to but don't want to lose money on either side, then it's perfect. 7. Are you working with a sponsor or recruiter? The person who introduced you to this business opportunity could determine to a large extent, your success or failure. In addition to the company being strong and successful, you also require coaching, training and motivation, and your sponsor would be useful with that. Recruiters tend to abandon people as soon as they sign them.

What are the top 100 MLM and Direct Selling Companies? Who is the No 1 MLM company in the world?

Every multi-level marketing (MLM) company in the world aims to expand its customer base and garner the highest-possible revenues. However, only a select few manage to attain this status. In the world of network marketing, finding success is easy in the initial stages of promoting a business or a product. Staying successful in the long run is a different ballgame, altogether.

Thousands of MLM companies from different parts of the world have announced their success stories. And, we've listed down the best of them. The most successful network marketing companies in 2020 have several things in common. But, they primarily showcase their strife to stay in the network marketing business for the past decade or more. These network marketing companies are likely to have a promising future in the direct selling industry over the upcoming decade.

Before we take a look at the top 100 network marketing companies of 2020, let's have the five key global leaders in the MLM domain.

Right Network Marketing Business

Top 5 Network Marketing Companies of the World in 2020

These top players in the global network marketing industry are retaining their leading positions for the past decade. These MLM companies are focused on growing customer base and allowing independent entrepreneurs in business growth by using their networks.

MLM has always been about providing network marketing salesforce to businesses or products. These top 5 network marketing companies are primarily concentrated towards providing their networks to healthcare and personal care businesses. They've supported entrepreneurs, gained the trust of customers, and symbolized reliability in their journey so far.

5 Nu Skin

Net Worth – US$ 4.68 Billion (as of 2018)

Nu Skin Enterprises is a leading US multi-level marketing company, operating mainly in North America and South America. With a network of 1.2 million independent marketeers, it distributes and sells dietary supplements and personal care products. It has established products under its Pharmanex brand. The Nu Skin network marketing diaspora is spread across 54 markets and over 500 marketplaces.

4 Herbalife

Net Worth – US$ 4.9 Billion (as of 2018)

One of the oldest in the business, Herbalife has gained an iconic position in the network marketing industry. Despite being levied into global trade controversies, the MLM company stays unbeatable with its sales of nutritional products. It gained US$250 Million net worth in 1996, becoming the pioneering success in the network marketing industry.

3 Avon

Net Worth – US$ 5.5 Billion (as of 2018)

In 2018, Avon and Avon Products generated annual sales worth over US$ 5 Billion value, becoming the world's fifth-largest company in beauty care. Currently, Avon operates in MLM front with over 6.4 million sales representatives. Due to its aggressive marketing strategies, it is dubbed to be the second-fastest direct selling company in the world, after Amway, in terms of sales growth.

2 Market America

Net Worth – US$ 7.3 Billion (as of 2018)

Despite facing a federal racketeering lawsuit in recent times, Market America leads the MLM competitive landscape by bringing in billion-dollar annual sales revenues from each of its operating markets. It operates in Australia, Singapore, China, Taiwan, Mexico, Spain, and Canada. It is also interesting to know that Market America bags the second spot in this list with a global sales force of just 180,000 representatives.

1 Amway

Net Worth – US$ 8.8 Billion (as of 2018)

Hands down, Amway is the biggest MLM company of all time! It has dominated the network marketing industry for the past fifteen years. Along with its sister concern – Alticor – Amway soars ahead by being the only MLM company to have the highest number of business partnerships and affiliated companies. Its million-strong sales force operates in more than 100 countries around the world.

The 2020 List of Top 100 MLM Companies in the World

The following list ranks the 100 best MLM & Direct Selling companies of 2020, based on 2019 revenues. The list also provided their estimated net worths as of 2019-end.

2020 Rank Company 2019 Revenue
1 Amway US$ 8.8 Billion
2 Market America US$ 7.3 Billion
3 Avon Products Inc. US$ 5.5 Billion
4 Herbalife US$ 4.9 Billion
5 Nu Skin US$ 4.6 Billion
6 Infinitus US$ 4.5 Billion
7 Vorwerk US$ 4.3 Billion
8 Natura US$ 3.6 Billion
9 Pharmaex US$ 2.6 Billion
10 Coway US$ 2.5 Billion
11 Tupperware US$ 2 Billion
12 Young Living US$ 1.9 Billion
13 Oriflame Cosmetics US$ 1.5 Billion
14 Rodan + Fields US$ 1.5 Billion
15 Jeunesse US$ 1.4 Billion
16 Ambit Energy US$ 1.3 Billion
17 DXN Marketing Sdn Bhd US$ 1.2 Billion
18 Pola US$ 1.2 Billion
19 O Boticário US$ 1.2 Billion

20 USANA Health Sciences US$ 1.1 Billion
21 Belcorp US$ 1.1 Billion
22 Atomy US$ 1.1 Billion
23 Telecom Plus US$ 1 Billion
24 Yanbal International US$ 995 Million
25 Shop.COM US$ 840 Million
26 PM International US$ 835 Million
27 Stream US$ 800 Million
28 Team National US$ 735 Million
29 Amore Pacific US$ 600 Million
30 Arbonne International US$ 545 Million
31 Hinode US$ 530 Million
32 Plexus US$ 530 Million
33 OPTAVIA / Medifast, Inc. US$ 500 Million
34 Miki US$ 500 Million
35 Faberlic US$ 465 Million
36 Scentsy US$ 450 Million
37 Monat Global US$ 435 Million
38 Younique US$ 430 Million
39 For Days US$ 385 Million
40 WorldVentures US$ 375 Million
41 Cosway US$ 365 Million
42 Nature's Sunshine US$ 365 Million
43 Prüvit US$ 325 Million
44 Beautycounter US$ 325 Million
45 Life Research US$ 325 Million
46 LG Household & Healthcare US$ 305 Million
47 Family Heritage Life US$ 295 Million
48 Vivint US$ 290 Million
49 Noevir US$ 275 Million
50 Hy Cite Enterprises, LLC US$ 275 Million
51 Pro-Partner US$ 245 Million
52 Pure Romance US$ 240 Million
53 Naturally Plus US$ 235 Million
54 New Image Group US$ 230 Million
55 proWIN International US$ 230 Million
56 Morinda US$ 230 Million
57 Menard US$ 225 Million

58 CUTCO/Vector Marketing US$ 225 Million
59 ARIIX US$ 225 Million
60 SEACRET US$ 210 Million
61 Southwestern Advantage US$ 205 Million
62 LifeVantage US$ 200 Million
63 Vida Divina US$ 195 Million
64 KK Assuran US$ 195 Million
65 Vestige Marketing US$ 195 Million
66 NHT Global US$ 190 Million
67 Hillary's Blinds US$ 185 Million
68 Giffarine Skyline Unity Co. US$ 180 Million
69 BearCere'Ju US$ 180 Million
70 Mannatech US$ 175 Million
71 Youngevity US$ 165 Million
72 Princess House US$ 160 Million
73 Charle US$ 155 Million
74 Diana US$ 145 Million
75 Naris US$ 135 Million
76 Maruko US$ 130 Million
77 Marketing Personal US$ 125 Million
78 Immunotec Research Ltd US$ 120 Million
79 ASEA US$ 120 Million
80 Color Street US$ 115 Million
81 World Global Network US$ 115 Million
82 Usborn Books & More US$ 115 Million
83 C'BON Cosmetics US$ 110 Million
84 Xyngular US$ 105 Million
85 TruVision Health US$ 105 Million
86 Zhulian US$ 105 Million
87 Nefful US$ 105 Million
88 MyDailyChoice / HempWorx US$ 100 Million
89 Perfectly Posh US$ 100 Million
90 Energetix US$ 95 Million
91 ZURVITA US$ 95 Million
92 Arsoa Honsha US$ 90 Million
93 Best World Int'l Ltd US$ 85 Million
94 Hai-O US$ 85 Million
95 Koyo-sha US$ 85 Million

96 Shinsei US$ 80 Million
97 Captain Tortue US$ 75 Million
98 Chandeal US$ 70 Million
99 Grant E One's US$ 65 Million
100 Nikken US$ 65 Million

FOUR
NETWORK MARKETING STRATEGY THAT WORKS

To really succeed in this industry you need to use a network marketingstrategy that is proven to bring results. Save yourself years of trialand error by using proven methods that have been pioneered by theindustry"s top earners.Most people new to network marketing don"t even thing about a network marketing strategy when they first open their business. Aftersigning on the dotted line, purchasing some product and a distributorkit, they plunge ahead without any training, planning or goal setting.Almost all the time, the person fails and then blames the networkmarketing industry, when it is really not the fault of networkmarketing.I notice that many people do not treat network marketing like a realbusiness. Any real business that you would open in your own communitywould have a business plan, and a marketing plan. Your networkmarketing business is the same.An effective network marketing strategy requires that you think long,hard and seriously about what it actually takes to succeed in thebusiness. No matter what company you are in, your strategy will alwaysinclude these three components

Leverage
Simplicity
Duplication

Many people are scared away from network marketing, also known as multi-level marketing (MLM), because of all the myths and misunderstanding about this type of business. Part of negativity comes from reported low MLM success rates.1 However, a multi-level marketing business isn't destined to fail any more than any other business. Regardless of the home business, you start, success comes from doing the work to build it.

For some reason, many people don't view their MLM business as a business, like they would if they opened a franchise or started a business from scratch. One of the most important things you can do to ensure your success is to treat your MLM venture as the business it is.

To stay safe from pyramid schemes and MLM scams, arm yourself with knowledge. Learn about the direct sales industry as a whole, research MLM companies carefully, and determine if you're a good match with your sponsor. The truth is, while you can get rich in MLM, statistics show that less than one out of 100 MLM representatives actually achieve MLM success or make any money.1 However, that's not necessarily the MLM business' fault. Most athletes never make it to the Olympics, but that's not sport's or the Olympics' fault.

Any great feat requires knowledge and action.

Find a Company With a Product You Love

Too many people get caught up in the hype of potential big income from MLM, that they don't pay enough attention to what the company is asking you to sell. You can't sell something or share your business if you don't genuinely have pride in what you are representing. Do your MLM research and partner with a company that has a product you can get excited about. Don't forget to look into the company's compensation plan before you join and make sure it is favorable to you.2

Be Genuine and Ethical

One reason that direct selling gets a bad rap is that many representatives use hype and sometimes deception to lure in new recruits.3 This leads many to believe that the MLM companies themselves encourage this behavior when in truth, they don't.

Legitimate MLM companies want you to be honest in your dealings with customers and potential recruits. If you love your product, your enthusiasm is enough to promote it. Just make sure you're not over-the-top or making exaggerated or false claims.

Nothing will annoy your family and cost you and friends, more than constantly pestering them about your business. There's nothing wrong with letting them know what you're doing and seeing if they have an interest, but if the answer is "no," let it go.

Many companies suggest making a list of 100 people you know, and while that's not wrong, you should consider that most successful MLMers have very few people from their original list of 100 people in their business. In most cases, friends and family who are in the business often come AFTER seeing the MLMer's success. Success in MLM comes from treating it like any other business in which you focus on the people who want what you have to offer. That means deciding who the target market is for your productsservices, as well as the business opportunity.

One of the biggest mistakes new MLMers make is looking at everyone (including friends and family as a potential customer or recruit.This is one area where the MLM industry gets it wrong. Like any other business, you're going to have greater success and efficiency if you identify your target market and focus your marketing efforts at them.

Many MLM sponsors will have you focus on recruiting new business builders; however, your income, in legitimate MLM, comes from the sales of products or services (whether through you or your recruits).5 Further, customers who love the products or services can more easily be converted into new business builders.

Just like any other business (home-based or otherwise), getting the word out about your product or service can benefit your target market is the key to generating new customers and recruits. Some ideas include sharing a product sample, inviting a neighbor to host a product party, or starting a website or social media account.

Know Your Target Market Very Well

To be great in what you want to do, you must know your well and gauge how best suited they are for small business opportunities. Be sure to keep in touch with their innermost desires and their needs. You need to understand what drives your audience in life and how they wish to improve their lifestyle.

You need to look at your audience as not only spectators but as people who have different needs and interests. One thing that can help you do this is to always keep an eye out for the monitoring dashboard.

If you know the people interested in leading a different and more satisfying life, this knowledge will rapidly enhance your network marketing.

Make Sure You Have Your "Why" Established

It is very important to acknowledge why you decided to become a network marketer. This WHY is your major driving force and the reason you have chosen this field.

The reason for choosing this field could be anything. It can be your family, your need to gain financial freedom, or have some free time in your hand. Make sure your reason is very strong. You can write down your list of reasons on a piece of paper and keep it in a safe place. You can take a look at it on the days when you feel low or face speed bumps in every corner.

You have to make sure your 'Why' is big enough to drive you until the end. If that's not the case, you don't have much scope in succeeding in this field.

Do Not Chase Your Family or Friends

Not many know this tactic, but one of the first things that network marketing companies ask you to do is prepare a list that includes all your friends and family members. This list will help you reach out to your near ones with your home-bound business goals. This list of your close ones is called the warm market segment.

The worst thing that can happen here your personal life and friendships would make your future meetings awkward.

It is best if you leave your friends and family away for a little while. Just keep them tucked away until you are able to understand prospects regarding network marketing and recruiting.

If you are lucky enough to support an experienced network marketer, then don't think twice and just go for it.

Let's make this very clear right from the start. When you are dealing with any member from the warm market segment, you don't ever have to chase, beg, guilt or attempt to convince anyone to be part of your opportunity.

As per your discretion, and when the time is right warranting your approach, you can check to see if your family or friends are willing to try out your small business home-based opportunity.

As a professional network marketer, you should never chase your family members or friends or even attempt to convince them to take interest in this opportunity.

Choose a Couple of Marketing Strategies to Master at a Time

The best way to understand network marketing strategies is by taking baby steps. Don't push yourself to learn and accomplish several marketing projects at the same time. Just like other network marketing businesses, you have a learning curve to overcome here as well, so just be patient.

It is not uncommon for people to get discouraged when they don't get what they had planned. With sheer patience and perseverance, you will overcome success and accomplish your business goals.

An easy way to go about this is to keep an eye on what other successful network marketing experts are doing. Observe their patterns and take your time to learn from how they have approached success. By doing this, you will soon be able to mimic the habits of a successful marketing professional. Soon enough, you, too, will begin to think and act like one. Doing this regularly can have a positive impact on your overall success rate.

Always remember that you are not alone in this. If you find yourself stuck in a roadblock along the way, don't force yourself to deal with it all by yourself. Simply contact your upline for whatever help you need.

Don't Ever Stop Learning or Educating Yourself

Each day, you have to put aside time so that you can work on yourself.

Did you know how top leaders and income earners in today's network marketing reached where they are?

Apart from mastering basic skills, they never stopped educating themselves. They are also tagged as the world's top earners.

All the popular network marketing professionals enjoy reading, and they follow a daily ritual to improve themselves. Just run a quick internet search on these readers and you will uncover that they all have a large bookshelf that makes them accomplished readers.

You can take the example of an expert you look up to. Lookup anyone who has money in this network marketing industry, and you will know how seriously they work on their personal development every day. You will also discover how they always have a library to keep their minds sharp, aware, and updated.

In conclusion, if you want to see visible improvement in your marketing efforts, make sure you are constantly improving your knowledge reservoirs. Always keep reading success books and ransack the internet for proven social media strategies. And while you are at it, don't forget to update yourself on any other topics that can pave the way toward your success.

Make Social Media an Essential Part of Your Everyday Business Activities

Even in the 21st century, if you still feel skeptical about what wonders social media marketing can do, then you've truly not understood its power yet. Social media marketing can help you increase your business exposure. Several digital marketers can attest that social media marketing plays a key role in driving traffic to your website and that it is as important as SEO.

If your online business is not accompanied by a social media strategy, you are already running into loss. A good social media promotion can help in spreading the word about your business to far-fetched people.

Including social media strategy in your daily business activities can form a base for a good marketing strategy. While there are many online portals you can start with to build your business relationships, a great place, to begin with, is Facebook. You can create Facebook groups within your niche to promote your business.

Consistency can help you reach great heights in all fields of life, including network marketing. All you need to do is create a plan and write it down on a to-do list to remain consistent. Try to be as consistent as possible in your actions because, without it, your business will fail.

Also, keep in mind, when you are posting content, consistency is the key. When your followers see that you post consistently, they will begin to expect it. Regular posting can also have a positive impact on SEO rankings with search engines. To gain a loyal follower base, try to remain consistent.

One shall remember, giving up is not the solution here, even if you don't see the results you want in your network marketing business.

Concluding: Marketing Secrets of the Network Marketing Experts

Don't take these secrets of becoming a network marketing expert lightly. Although they may seem very small to begin with, they have made grounds for greatness.

Remember that all these marketing tips are not enough to create a windfall of leads. Creating a network marketing business will take its own time to evolve, so you cannot expect overnight success in it.

It is possible to achieve success in network marketing if you can follow these pieces of advice and start implementing them right away. Soon enough, you will be able to witness drastic changes in your small business.

Network Marketing Strategy That Works

FIVE

START YOUR NETWORK MARKETING BUSINESS

Taking Responsibility Success is up to you. If you succeed in this business, it will be because you made a decision to make something happen. Failure is up to you. It's not up to anyone else – it's up to you. You alone will decide whether you succeed or fail. Your sponsor is simply your connection to the company. The truth is, that most of the top earners in network marketing didn't have a very good upline. If you have an upline that does everything for you, then you don't have to become much. Use your sponsor as a resource, but not as an excuse. Decide to become independent as quick as you can. It's always helpful to have a "workout partner" in your business; a person you can relate to, somebody who motivates you and inspires you. It doesn't matter where this person is in your company. They might be in an upline, a downline or even a crossline. The most important thing is you will keep each other accountable.

Expectations – Managing the Emotions Network marketing is a very emotional business. There will be ups and downs. Life will distract you, and throw things in your way to try to get you back into that daily grind. You'll face rejection from ignorant people. Most people are completely ignorant to network marketing. They think they get it, but they don't. They mostly have a misconception of network marketing. They think everyone at the top makes most of the money, that you have to alienate your family and friends and that you have to push inferior products. None of this is true. People will quit. Your group will be attacked. You will either fight and keep building, or quit the business yourself. Your past will punish or reward you at the beginning. If you've lived a good life, been a giver, been helpful to other people, a good friend to other people, those people are naturally going to look at what you have. If you've been a taker your whole life, people will hesitate to look at what you're presenting. Early in my career, I was primarily a taker. People were skeptical when I suddenly had interest in their life. You can turn this around. You can start to be a giver.

How To Get Involved in Your Business Commit yourself to doing this right. Your story of how you get involved is really important. Are you just trying it, or are you really serious? Did you sign up with the smallest or the highest package? Let me explain why it is important. You're going to be telling the story of how you got started for the rest of your career. When people ask you how you started, will you be able to tell them you got started at the highest possible level? This isn't like starting a traditional business. You don't have to make a huge investment, design logos, hire lawyers, sign a lease, or anything traditional business owners need to do. If you start with the best possible package, that is the story you'll tell for the rest of your network marketing career. It's the one you want everyone in your group to have. It shows your commitment. You're not just testing the water. Make a solid monthly commitment. Whether it's a product or autoship, make sure it's solid and duplicable. Introduce yourself to everyone. When I went to my first convention, I made a commitment to introduce myself to everyone there. I can't tell you how much difference that made. It helped create circles of friends in the business that I could also go to for support in difficult times. Build a community, make friends and connections. These friends and connections are not tied to you financially, as your upline is. They will be tremendously helpful to you as you build your business.

Business Details

The tax benefits to starting your network marketing business are enormous! Talk to your tax professional. If you do this right, you will see tremendous benefits. To see the most benefit, track expenses and keep receipts. Keep good accounts, and consider having a separate account for your business. As a network marketing business-builder, you're an independent contractor, so you'll need to save for taxes. Your tax advisor can tell you how much of each check should be paid in for taxes. And one more piece of advice: If you have the ability, I'd encourage you to NOT spend your Network Marketing money. Have that be your future, your retirement, your retire your spouse fund – have it be something else. Let's say you have enough to pay your bills with your "job." Let the network marketing money become your financial freedom. Use this to create your future. The biggest status symbol today is being debt-free. If you just use your network marketing money to become debt-free, that would be amazing.

Let's Get Your Business Going

One of the first things to do is to make your active candidate list. (Make sure you download the Ultimate Memory Jogger workbook.) Add as many people as you can to your list. I hope you'll start today. If you haven't downloaded the Memory Jogger, just start with the lines below and start writing. Go! Add at least 2 people every day. Adding people to your list is a muscle that is developed by successful network marketers.

Inviting Basics In my book Go Pro, you'll find the basics on inviting people to your opportunity. And as part of this program, you'll receive my basic script book. They will help you learn about the different markets you'll face. You have a hot market (close friends and family), a warm market (people you "sort of " know), and a cold market – people you don't know at all. But please! Please, before you start, learn the "support and practice" approach. Don't mention your new business to anyone before you learn these skills. You don't want to "verbally vomit" on the people who are most likely to buy from you, even if you're super excited for your chance for a future. It's easy to go overboard. Learn the "support and practice" approach and use it, use it, use it! You're free to make mistakes with the people who love you the most. It doesn't have to be perfect. They can see the opportunity and if they aren't interested, you can just ask for their support in becoming a customer or using the product. Learn invitation basics. There are direct, indirect, and super indirect approaches. Details are in the book, but here are the steps to a professional invitation. Step one: Be in a hurry. Step two: Compliment the prospect Step three: Make the invitation Step four: If I, would you? Step five: Confirmation #1 - get the time commitment Step six: Confirmation #2 - confirm the time commitment Step seven: Confirmation #3 - schedule the next call Step eight: Get off the phone.

The Launch Proclaim yourself. Go tell the world that you're part of the company and you're going to the top. It makes it a little more embarrassing for you to walk away. It's really important. It's like opening a restaurant. You'd be inviting your friends and family to check out your food, the ambiance and atmosphere, and you'd be asking them to tell their friends.

The same thing is true with your network marketing business. Treat it like a race. You want to get going fast and build some buzz and momentum. You want them to help you launch your business properly.

start your network marketing business

Your Product Story

It will be important for you to get your product story fast. What did the product do for you? You need to get product sales and customers fast. This will help you get new distributors signed up fast. "I did this, and it created this result." The more you tell your story, the more quickly your business will succeed.

Network marketing success is built in 15-minute increments. If you're busy with your life, just carve out 15 minutes to make phone calls. Carve out 15 minutes to show someone the product or opportunity. This will help you create a daily method of operation that will give you results and income. "

Time Management

A lot of people feel they don't have enough time to start a new business. They don't think they have any additional time to build a business. Don't treat this like a business. Treat it like a job where you have specific hours and you have to perform in those hours. When people join network marketing they sometimes treat it way too casually. Don't let small things take you off your game. Network marketing success is built in 15-minute increments. If you're busy with your life, just carve out 15 minutes to make phone calls. Carve out 15 minutes to show someone the product or opportunity. In real life, most people don't put in 10 hours of real work at their office. A lot of the time in an office is spent doing things that are unproductive, time-wasting behaviors. Real work, total focus, can be done in forty 15-minute blocks. This will help you create a daily method of operation that will give you results, encouragement, income – all are created by your daily habits. All of us are slaves to our habits, good or bad. I encourage you to become a slave to good habits. Don't let things steal your time, become a person who purposefully uses time. If you're a slave to television, limit your television. Are you a slave to email or social media? Understand, you don't have to constantly react to everyone's agenda. Take charge. Treat it like a job. Work through the steps of what's taking your time, and what will help you build a future. Decide what is important for you.

Personal Development

This is so important. In the end you only make what you are. You only earn what you become as a person. To have more you have to become more. Work on yourself harder than you work on your business. You are the only barrier to higher income. If you want to do more, you need to become more. Things that will help you: Your reading library. What are you reading? Take 15-30 minutes a day to read one thing that will help you be a better leader, motivator, teacher. Your reading library is super important. Leaders are readers. Your listening library. Listen to people like Jim Rohn, Les Brown, Denis Waitley. Listen to books on audio. Fill your mind with great ideas from people who have gone before you. Your viewing library. What are you watching? More people watch You Tube than watch television or read magazines. I put a lot of free videos up on Network Marketing Pro.

There are some great inspirational people on some of these videos. Another great site is ted.com. Some of the greatest leaders of the world give talks on these videos. Attending events. These will help you grow your business and develop you personally. Events fill you up. Whether it's a Network Marketing Pro event, a Dale Carnegie or Anthony Robbins event, your company or regional events – these will fill you up. Have these be part of your personal development plan.

Focus & Consistency

Network Marketing is filled with distractions. Put the blinders on and commit. Take things one year at a time, not a day at a time. Commit to the next 12 months and make it happen. Evaluate. Commit to another 12 months. Evaluate. Make it happen. Stay on track. Focus where you are. Follow the people in your company who are having the biggest success. Do what they do. Look at what's working and commit to getting better in that process.

The Importance of Events

Commit now to attending all major company events. It changed everything for me when I committed to never missing a company convention. It became about how resourceful I could be, to raise the money to get to that event. All of the life-changing experiences I have had in network marketing have occurred because I attended company events. Register for your company event now. Make that commitment. It will change everything. Make sure everybody on your team registers and attends company events. Explain to them why it's so important. Work on the plan and help as many people as you can to attend the big event.

Stories Stories will help you build your business. Why did you decide to pursue network marketing? What in your background prepared you for a career in this profession? Be able to tell this story in a couple of minutes. You should also have a "getting started" story. What helped you get started? Did you attend some training? Eliminate distractions? Talking about your getting started process can be incredibly inspiring. Your product story is also very important. We touched on that a little earlier. When you used the product or service, what happened? How did that product or service benefit you? In telling your story, people will see how it will also benefit them. Have a "first 30-day" story. What happened in your first 30 days? It will inspire people to what they can do in their first 30 days. People remember stories way more than they remember the data or statistics. Stories carry impact. Pay attention to your stories, and work on them. Become a good storyteller.

Focus on Skills

This is my strongest recommendation! I finally decided to be a professional after spending three-and-a-half years in network marketing. Your skills will make a career for you. You'll never have to worry about being lucky or waste time looking for shortcuts again. As a part of this program, Network marketing pro has offered you two additional tools that will help you so much with the skills: - Memory Jogger workbook - Script book Use these products to help you develop necessary skills. The "Go Pro" book is an amazing additional tool. If you didn't read it yet, you have to read it. Hundreds of thousands of distributors around the world are using it with great success.

Massive Success Can Be Yours I want you to get the results you're looking for and understand what we have. And pass it on to other people. There are three things you need to do to have massive success in the network marketing profession. 1: Have a solid understanding of the gift that we have of network marketing – being able to be an entrepreneur without a huge investment, and being able to expand outside of your geography. 2: Master the skills. They're not hard. You have to work at them, but they're learnable. 3: Face your fears - of inadequacy, of rejection, of the unknown. Once you have a strong understanding and skills, the fear dissipates. It's like flipping on a light switch! When you master the skills, your fear will disappear

SIX
11 Tips to Help You Network Better!

Networking. Everyone does it but how do you do it well?

Many people believe that networking during a job search means calling everyone and asking them for a job. People associate networking with being pushy and overbearing. Some people tend to hide away from networking because they don't want to be labeled as this type of person. Networking is a two way street, it is a way of getting to know someone better and finding ways they might be able to help you and how you can help them in return. Click here to see full list of TAFE courses.

A professional networking event is a great opportunity to present yourself, make new connections and even find yourself a new job. Current research shows that a large number of jobs are filled through networking. Successful networkers display a sincere interest in their networking contacts and work hard to develop a relationship, establish their credibility and share their information and knowledge. To become a successful networker, you should follow the belief that everyone has something to learn and gain.

Networking is an ongoing process, it requires persistence, attention, organisation and good will. Incorporate the art of networking into your job search and you will gain opportunities and build relationships that will last a lifetime. Demonstrate your value to potential clients and employers with these simple successful networking tips:

1. Meet People Through Other People

The best and easiest way to meet people is through referrals. Stick around with the people you already know and who know the people you are looking to meet. Being introduced through them or joining in with their conversations you will very likely receive a warm welcome and introduction to the person you wanted an introduction to. This is a similar effect to LinkedIn through their online introduction tool, or even through joining the right circle at an event with somebody you know.

Networking is the exchange of information and ideas among people with a common profession or special interest, usually in an informal social setting. Networking often begins with a single point of common ground.

Professionals use networking to expand their circles of acquaintances, find out about job opportunities in their fields, and increase their awareness of news and trends in their fields or the greater world.

2. Leverage Social Media

Social media is an effective way to get to know important contacts better and without the pressure of a face to face meeting that you may not be prepared for. Seek out like-minded or key contacts you would like to know better within your LinkedIn profile, Google Plus, Twitter and more. Try commenting on a link they post or responding to a comment they make, start a conversation with them and offer them value in return. When you have the opportunity to meet them in person it will be easier to reference previous communications with them.

3. Don't Ask For A Job

Networking is not asking everyone you know for a job, in fact, when you network you should never ask someone for a job. You should ask people for information that will assist you in your job search. Your main networking goal should be to build a relationship and establish rapport so when a potential opportunity may arise in the future, your contact may be willing to refer you.

4. Use Your Resume as a Tool for Advice

Another easy yet highly effective way to network during a job search is to ask others who you have established a relationship with to review your resume and give you feedback on how to improve it. Using this technique is valuable for a number of reasons. When reviewing your resume they will discover your work history, your previous titles, your objectives and many things they may not yet know about you. They may remember a company or a connection that your background may be perfectly suited to.

5. Don't Take Up Too Much Time

Before you start networking, be sure to have an agenda and keep the meeting on track. Time is money and people are never happy with someone that takes up too much of their time. By planning out your meeting ahead of time, you establish your professionalism, you gain credibility and cover all the critical topics you wanted to cover. .

6. Let The Other Person Speak

When networking, be sure that you don't do all the talking. The key to being a good conversationalist is being a good listener. If you have asked another person for advice or their opinion, make sure they have the opportunity to offer it and tell you. Or perhaps they are looking for you to add value to their work. If you do all the talking, the person may feel you are uninterested in what they have to say and unsure what action to take with the information you have supplied. Ask some of the following questions:

    How long have you been with this company? Or how long have you been in this field?
    What do you like or dislike about your job?
    What type of training did you need for this position?
    What is the culture of this company?

7. Present A Success Story

Once you have found a topic the other person may be interested in and you can offer advice on, present a solution by telling a story about how you helped other in a similar situation. Tell them about your problem and how you solved it, but keep it short and sweet. Start by telling them about the problem and then your solution. Include lots of information on how disastrous things were before it came to a happy ending, where everything worked out for the better."Success stories" are an important marketing tool for]project-open[. Success stories are usually directed towards potential customers who seriously consider using]project-open[for their organization. The success stories provide these readers with real-world examples, and help them to set expectations in terms of implementation time, budget etc. The readers are usually the managers or owners of service organizations.

8. Ask For Suggestions on How to Expand Your Network

One of the main goals of networking is not only to meet one or two people, but also to tap into the network of the people you are meeting with. Each separate person you meet will know approximately another 200 people, and if you can gain introductions to some of these contacts, you will quickly increase your network and your chances of finding an extremely valuable connection. Ask your contacts if they can recommend a professional organisation or the names of some of the people you should be talking with.

It's common knowledge that networking is an essential factor toward career success, but it's also easy to forget just how often we should be making the effort! If you've been working in your field for a couple of years, you probably already have some sort of established network. However, expanding your network can be difficult if you already struggle to network in general.

Deciding where to start can be overwhelming at first, but instead of viewing networking opportunities with trepidation, view them as opportunities for professional development. Before you know it, you'll get the hang of it and have an even more impressive network than you could have imagined!

9. Find a Reason to Follow Up

If you want to establish rapport with another person, create a reason to keep the relationship going. If you read an article that adds to a discussion you had during a networking meeting, save it and send it to them with a brief note on what you found interesting and how you think it could benefit them. Try and find at least two or three opportunities yearly to reconnect with the members of your network.

When you start a new business or release a new product, your primary focus is on spreading the word across the market and once that's done, potential customers pull up their socks to get associated with the new venture. But that is not the end of the story! No matter how many people you attract in the first place, they will never convert into your customers if timely follow-up on them is not fulfilled. As they say, agents who don't follow-up with customers are leaving a lot of money on the table.

When you start a new business or release a new product, your primary focus is on spreading the word across the market and once that's done, potential customers pull up their socks to get associated with the new venture. But that is not the end of the story! No matter how many people you attract in the first place, they will never convert into your customers if timely follow-up on them is not fulfilled. As they say, agents who don't follow-up with customers are leaving a lot of money on the table.

10. Always Remember to Say Thank You

Building a network is about creating a genuine, caring relationship. Thank your connection for the information they have given and see if you can help them in any way. Share any knowledge you feel would be useful for them. Keep notes on what you learn about your contacts so your future correspondence can have a personalised touch.

If you type a variation of "what do I need for my business to succeed" into a search engine, then you'll get somewhere in the neighborhood of one quintillion blog posts and articles promising an answer. You need a brand new website! No wait, you really need an automated chatbot! Or, just kidding, you really, really need a social media manager! If you don't mind, I'd like to tell you a secret: you only need one thing for your business to succeed. Ready?

Clients. You need clients.

Clients are the difference between "running a digital marketing agency" and "having a digital marketing hobby." Which I think we can all agree would be an odd choice for a hobby. When it comes down to it, the vast majority of business decisions are based around either getting more clients or keeping existing clients happy.

A new website will improve your online presence and help you reach a wider audience and make a better impression on potential clients.

Hiring a new employee that will allow you to expand your business offerings will improve your existing clients' experiences.

An awesome, regularly updated blog will impress your readers and hopefully bring in some new clients.

All told, well-maintained client relationships will separate a successful small business from a really expensive and stressful hobby. So, let's talk about establishing positive client relationships.

Relationships take work.

Even the phrase "client relationship" gives us some direction. As a rule, relationships are meaningful, preferably long-term, and require regular maintenance to thrive. Client relationships are no different. At Spring Insight, we're all about long-term client relationships. Marketing is a long game, and we see our best results when we get to work with clients over the long term. As far as maintenance goes, doing consistent and good work is the foundation of a good relationship. But it's not the only piece of the puzzle.

It's also important that your clients understand that you're thankful for them. Please note that I said "thankful for them," not "thankful for their business," or "thankful for their money." Although let's be real, business and money are pretty great. But, being thankful for your clients is about more than revenue. It's about being thankful for their trust, thankful for the constructive feedback that makes you better, and thankful for all the nice things they say about you to their peers.

Show. Don't tell.

How do you show that you're thankful for your clients? You start by treating them in a way that makes it clear how much you value them. You do the little things right, like respond promptly and address concerns respectfully. But, it doesn't hurt to send a tangible "thanks!" every now and then. For example, by sending a client appreciation gift.

"Oh great! I send holiday gifts every single year," you say. Cool. So does everyone else. Your gift, no matter how well-intentioned, isn't going to stand out in the sea of gift baskets, candy, and thoughtful cards clogging up your clients' entryways. If you want your client appreciation gift to stand out, you're really left with two choices. You can either A) get super creative or B) consider sending your gift at a different time of year.

If you go with option A, I'm very interested in what you decide to send. I appreciate a gift that can stand out in a crowd. At Spring Insight, we go with option B. We send our client appreciation gifts the week before spring starts every year (get it!). The exact gift is different every year, obviously, but is always:

Branded (hey, it is generous, but it is still marketing.)

Spring themed (or at least we try but to be honest, we are running dry. Ideas anyone?)

Something people will actually use (we hate swag that has no utility. Don't you?)

Awesome (duh)

But, no matter what we decide to send, it will always come in bright purple packaging, because the world needs more purple. Also, because it is a Spring Insight color. More importantly, the gift always comes with a handwritten note. It's my chance to express my gratitude and make sure my clients understand just how thankful I am for them.

I hope that you're feeling inspired to remind your clients how much you appreciate them. And, if you would like a few more clients to thank this time next year, get in touch. The marketing team at Spring Insight is here to help.

11. *Online Presence*

Ensure your online profile is always up-to-date. Recruiters often use social media platforms to probe potential candidates, and even to check out your skills and experience.

These few basic rules will help you succeed at networking. Remember, the goal at networking is to build relationships and networks. A good, reliable network can result in new customers, partners and opportunities. Get out there and meet people, but ensure you are following these networking tips to make sure you are meeting people in the right way.

The other day I was trying to find the perfect dress pant yoga pants because I wanted comfortable, professional clothing options.

When I searched for "dress pant yoga pants" on Google, I found the brand Betabrand.

Amazingly, the company dominated the top four search results. The first two results were their website, the third was their Amazon page, and the fourth was a review of their product.

Deciding I wanted to look into it further, I searched for Betabrand on Google and found their social media pages, a Wikipedia page, their website, their Amazon store, and reviews.

They were impossible to ignore online. Ultimately, I ended up making a purchase.

My buyer's journey is not unique.

In fact, according to Adaptive Marketing, 97% of consumers use the internet to find a business.

That's why having an online presence is important.

It helps consumers find your brand before they are aware you exist and it helps them learn about your reputation before making a purchase. Eventually, all of this information will play a role in your customer's purchasing decision.

Below we'll review what an online presence is, and explore 16 effective ways to build your online presence.

1. Build an email list.

One of the top ways to build your online presence is to create and grow an email list. An email list will enable you to engage with current and potential customers on a daily, weekly, or monthly basis.

To grow your email list, you can create gated content that users have to sign-up to receive. Additionally, you can use a call-to-action (CTA) on your website and social media pages to promote your email newsletter. With a newsletter, you're able to collect leads' emails -- additionally, it shows your leads and customers are interested in your content.

You can use tools in your content management system (CMS) to create forms, slide-in CTAs, or popups that are designed to gather email addresses. For example, HubSpot offers an email marketing tool, free pop-up forms, and a free online form builder to help build an email list. Alternatively, you might consider checking out MailChimp or GetResponse.

2. Master SEO.

With algorithms changing every day, search engine optimization (SEO) is one of the best tactics to build your online presence.

The first step to showing up online when people are searching is to master SEO.

SEO can be divided into two categories -- on-site SEO, and off-site SEO.

On-site SEO is all about the content. You'll want to use keyword research, include internal and external links, and create educational content that likely matches your target audiences' search queries.

With off-site SEO, you'll pay attention to the more technical side of things. For example, you'll want to make sure your site is set up correctly, has simple URL structuring, and loads quickly. Additionally, off-site SEO also includes building credibility with backlinks.

Lastly, if you want to show up on Google, create a Google My Business account, and use Google's keyword planner.

3. Create value.

Overall, your brand or company's goal is to make money. But before you can make money, you have to create value and be customer-centric.

One way to create value is to provide educational, free content online. Not only is this helpful for your customers, but it'll also improve your online presence.

To get started, write out a list of your customer's pain points and motivations. In other words, take a look at your buyer persona.

Then, brainstorm content that would answer their questions. What information would help your customers? This will be the basis for your content strategy.

Another way to create value online is to give advice. You could do this through guest posting, responding to comments, or appearing on a podcast. Wherever your customers have questions, you should be answering them.

4. Be active online.

In order to show up online, you have to be active online. This includes regularly posting to your owned properties, including your website and social media accounts.

Additionally, you should be active in other areas, as well. For example, you should engage with followers and subscribers on social media. If there's something that everyone is talking about in your industry, you can engage in the conversation.

5. Analyze your results.

Once you get started with a few tactics to build your online presence, it's critical you analyze your results. I would suggest testing your strategies so you learn what works and what doesn't.

In order to test your results, start out by deciding what metrics you're using. If you're working on your SEO, you might track your search engine results on Google. On the other hand, if you're building an email list, you might track the number of subscribers, plus your open and click-through rates.

Keep in mind that these are long-term strategies. Some may take time to produce results. Additionally,, some may be harder to track, like brand awareness. But that's okay -- just because results may be hard to track doesn't mean it's not worth doing.

6. Adopt new forums.

When new social media or popular websites emerge, be an early adopter. There are many benefits to being an early adopter.

First, if you're an early adopter, there's less competition. Second, most of these websites start out free and have high engagement rates.

To be an early adopter, make sure you're always in "the know." Read industry news and research new, up-and-coming sites.

7. Have a social media presence.

Being on social media is a necessity in this day and age. In fact, in 2019 there are now 3.2 billion people on social media globally, so social media is a key tool for reaching your intended audience on whichever platforms they prefer.

Having a presence on social media instills trust in your current customers and prospects. Personally, if I see that a company doesn't have a presence on social media, I lose trust and feel unsure if they even exist.

Plus, social media is a great way to build your credibility and reputation and showcase your brand. When potential customers are researching your brand, the first place they'll look is social media to see what you're putting out there and what people are saying about you.

8. Make a website.

Not to be repetitive, but again, to show up online, you have to have a website online. Besides social media, one of the first places people will go to find out more about your company is your website.

Your website is where you can show off your brand through colors, fonts, text, video, and images. You'll appeal to your buyer persona's pain points and present a solution to their problem.

To make a website, there are many CMS sites you can use, including HubSpot, Wix, WordPress, and Squarespace.

9. Produce content.

The more content you produce, the more opportunities you have to show up online. Having an online presence is all about showing up in search engines, on social media, and sites like YouTube.

To start producing content, strategize what places you want to show up online. Do you want to be on Facebook, Instagram, YouTube, Twitter,

Pinterest, Etsy, Poshmark, Goodreads, or Amazon?

Prioritize the sites your customers are active on (based on customer research) and start brainstorming content that is best-suited for those mediums.

For example, with YouTube, you'll come up with video ideas -- whereas on Instagram, you'll come up with photo and caption ideas.

10. Personify your brand.

Building an online presence is a lot like building a brand. One tactic many companies use to build a brand is to personify their brand.

For example, The Skimm, a daily newsletter, personified their brand when they were founded in 2012. The founders created a persona called The Skimm Girl. This was the personification of their brand. They knew her likes, dislikes, age, job, financial situation, and sense of humor.

By personifying their brand, the company was able to appeal to their target demographic while staying true to their mission and values.

Having a clear brand helps users relate to your company and makes them want to engage with you, whether through a social media comment or by signing up for your email newsletter.

11. Experiment with online advertising.

A faster solution to building an online presence is through online advertising. If your ad shows up in the top search results, you'll build brand awareness and increase your visibility online.

You can advertise on search engines like Google, Yahoo, and Bing. Additionally, you can look into social media advertising. Facebook, Instagram, and YouTube are well-known for their advertising options.

Before you begin advertising online, brainstorm what you want to promote. Do you want to promote a certain content offer? Alternatively, perhaps you want to advertise your email newsletter?

Once you choose what it is you want to advertise, you'll also need to decide on the platform that is best-suited (i.e. has the right audience) to promote that content on.

12. Research influencer marketing.

In order to stay active in your community, it's important to engage with the most popular figures in your niche.

For instance, if you sell beauty products, you might consider researching beauty influencers on YouTube and Instagram. Many consumers look to influencers for their honest reviews and promotion before purchasing a product.

Additionally, influencer marketing will get the word out about your brand online. The more people are talking about you, the more often you'll show up online.

13. Be competitive.

When you're building an online presence, remember to be competitive. Look at what your competitors are doing and discuss whether or not that's a good strategy for your business, as well.

You can also use your competitors to see what they're missing. Is there a gap they aren't filling? What information do customers want that your competitors aren't providing?

Researching your competitors should give you ideas for content and strategies. You won't be able to compete with or one-up your competitors if you aren't sure what they're doing.

14. Develop relationships.

Developing relationships with those in your industry is an important way to build your online presence.

For instance, if you have a relationship with blog writers or podcasters in your industry, they might feature you in their content. Perhaps they'll ask you to guest post or appear on their podcast.

Forging relationships with others in your industry will ultimately help you show up online.

15. Show up where your audience is.

To show up online, you have to figure out where your audience is.

If your audience is on Instagram, but they aren't on Twitter, you shouldn't be putting all your efforts into Twitter. On the contrary, you should be focusing your content and promotion strategy on Instagram.

If you show up where your audience is, you'll build a strong online presence that customers can't ignore.

16. Automate your process.

Lastly, building an online presence includes a lot of tedious tactics.

In order to ensure the system runs smoothly, automate some of your processes. For instance, you can schedule your content to go live on your CMS and social media.

Additionally, you can curate other people's content, which enables you to provide valuable resources for your audience without constantly creating fresh content.

You can also plan your email marketing newsletters in advance, and set up email sign-up forms on your site that show up automatically.

These marketing strategies can help you build your online presence, create brand awareness, and develop a strong reputation. Building an online presence requires effort, but over time it will pay off with increased sales and better brand awareness in your industry.

Make a great network

Networking Is The Exchange Of Information

Networking is used by professionals to widen their circles of acquaintances, find out about job opportunities, and increase their awareness of news and trends in their fields.

Business owners may network to develop relationships with people and companies they may do business with in the future.

Professional networking platforms provide an online location for people to engage with other professionals, join groups, post blogs, and share information.

The coronavirus pandemic drove many professionals to network solely online rather than in person.

Many colleges and universities provide opportunities for alumni to network with one another.

People generally join networking groups based on a single common point of interest that all members share. The most obvious is a professional affiliation, such as stockbrokers. Still, some people find effective networking opportunities in a college alumni group, a church or synagogue social group, or a private club.

For professionals, the best networking opportunities may occur at trade shows, seminars, and conferences, designed to attract a large crowd of likeminded individuals. Networking helps a professional keep up with current events in the field and develops relationships that may boost future business or employment prospects. Needless to say, it also provides opportunities to help other people find jobs, make connections, and catch up on the news.

Small business owners network to develop relationships with people and companies they may do business with in the future. These connections help them establish rapport and trust among people in their own communities. Successful business networking involves regularly following up with contacts to exchange valuable information that may not be readily available outside the network.

Professional networking platforms such as LinkedIn provide an online location for people to engage with other professionals, join groups, post blogs, and share information. And, of course, they provide a place to post a resume that can be seen by prospective employers, to search for jobs, or to identify job candidates.

These days, a business-to-business (B2B) customer pipeline can be developed almost entirely through the use of a social networking site. Online networking forums allow professionals to demonstrate their knowledge and connect with like-minded people.

LinkedIn is the largest professional network, but there are many others.1 Some cater to particular subsets of people, such as Black Business Women Online. Others have a different focus, such as Meetup, which encourages its members to meet in person off-site or virtually through online video conferences.

Given the growing number of networking opportunities available to people looking to start or advance their careers, it's important to take some time to explore your options before committing to a specific networking group.

While it's tempting for a new business owner or someone looking for a dream job to join as many networks as possible, a better strategy is to target your time and efforts toward those groups that best fit your needs and interests. Many networking organizations will host a special meet and greet events that allow potential new members to attend a meeting before becoming a member.

Once you join a networking group, it's important to become a contributing member. Rather than just using the association to further their own goals, people who use networking effectively look to offer something of value to other group members. Networking can help you identify opportunities for collaboration, strategic joint ventures, partnerships, and new areas to expand your business.

It's important to take some time to explore your options before committing to a specific networking group. While it's tempting for a new business owner or someone looking for a dream job to join as many networks as possible, a better strategy is to target your time and efforts toward those groups that best fit your needs and interests.

Many networking organizations will host a special meet and greet events that allow potential new members to attend a meeting before becoming members. Once you join a networking group, it's important to become a contributing member. Rather than just using the association to further their own goals, people who use networking effectively look to offer something of value to other group members.

Professionals use networking to expand their circles of acquaintances, find out about job opportunities in their fields, and increase their awareness

NETWORKING IS THE EXCHANGE OF INFORMATION

of news and trends in their fields or the greater world. It helps a professional keep up with current events in the field and develops relationships that may boost future business or employment prospects.

Small business owners network to develop relationships with people and companies they may do business with in the future. These connections help them establish rapport and trust among people in their own communities. Successful business networking involves regularly following up with contacts to exchange valuable information that may not be readily available outside the network.

Business owners and entrepreneurs often join their local chamber of commerce to promote their business interests and help others in their community do the same. Networking can help you identify opportunities for collaboration, strategic joint ventures, partnerships, and new areas to expand your business.

Professional networking platforms such as LinkedIn provide an online location for people to engage with other professionals, join groups, post blogs, and share information. And, of course, they provide a place to post a resume that can be seen by prospective employers, to search for jobs, or to identify job candidates. These days, a business-to-business (B2B) customer pipeline can be developed almost entirely through the use of a social networking site. Online networking forums allow professionals to demonstrate their knowledge and connect with like-minded people.

Attending networking events is a fantastic way to make business connections. The problem is, a lot of us can't stand the idea of networking. It feels fake and contrived. And if you're an introvert, fuggettaboutit.

Just thinking of spending hours on small talk in a loud and crowded room of strangers is enough to make you exhausted. But it doesn't have to be if you approach it the right way. Most people go to these types of events with the intent to push their agenda on anyone who will listen to them. Here are 10 tips to network without being fake.

Social media is an effective way to get to know important contacts better and without the pressure of a face to face meeting that you may not be prepared for. Seek out like-minded or key contacts you would like to know better within your LinkedIn profile, Google Plus, Twitter and more. Try commenting on a link they post or responding to a comment they make, start a conversation with them and offer them value in return. When you have the opportunity to meet them in person it will be easier to reference previous communications with them.

Social media was initially created with the idea of connecting people in the digital world. However, over the years, its purpose has diversified to a great extent. Today, it is one of the most powerful tools for businesses to connect and engage with their audiences. But, why is it so important to leverage social media for business?

Well, look at the numbers. A study by Sprout Social found that 60% of millennials are likely to purchase from a brand they follow online. The numbers are favorable even for other generations using social media. 67% of Gen X and 51% of baby boomers are likely to do the same.

This means that if you can get yourself noticed amidst all of the noise in the digital world, your business is bound to grow. In fact, leveraging social media for your business should be one of your top priorities.

By leveraging social media, you can also get more word-of-mouth recommendations and more traffic to your website. It can drive your profits too. However, the results will depend on how effective your social media marketing strategy is.

The good news is that leveraging social media for business is really not rocket science. You just need to know a few basic tricks. To help you with it, we've listed a few tips that will ensure you're moving in the right direction. Be patient and follow these pointers consistently. The results will soon follow.

Be it LinkedIn, Facebook, Twitter, or Instagram, your business needs to have a presence on one or more social channels. However, before you create your business accounts, think about where you are most likely to find your target audience.

If you are a B2B brand, you definitely need to be active on LinkedIn because it's your best chance of engaging with decision makers. On the other hand, if your products are more visually-stimulating, Instagram is definitely a great option. In general, platforms like Instagram or Snapchat are frequented by younger audiences. And Facebook is preferred by older ones.

So get to know your audience. Google Analytics can help you with this. You can get insights into age groups, locations, and other demographic data about your audiences using it.

Once you know your target market well, choose a suitable social media platform. Opt for the one which your target market uses the most.

Once you start posting, analyze which groups in your target audiences are responding well. Also analyze which social media platforms are giving you the most engagement. Keep a tab on the kind of content you're getting the most engagement from.

You can use Facebook and Instagram Insights, Twitter Analytics, and other such tools for this analysis. You'll be able to see your users' genders, locations, ages, interests, and a lot more. It's a goldmine of information that you can use to your advantage.

Pictures and videos may do well on Instagram, while long blog posts may perform better on LinkedIn. Experiment a little and see what works.

Accordingly, tweak your content to suit the platform that you're posting on. If you want to leverage social media for your business, you'll need to get creative. Also, think of multiple ways of posting the same content in different formats.

Of course, your goal is to sell. However, you can't be blatant about it on social media. Show, don't tell. Weave a visual story around your brand, but don't aggressively sell your products or services. Good storytelling will help you connect better with your target audiences.

Take some inspiration from Airbnb's Instagram posts. They have beautiful pictures, and each post is accompanied by an engaging caption. They describe the place and the experience it provides. They even capture the lives of locals.

Each of their posts beautifully supports their core value – "Embrace the adventure." Instead of directly selling their brand, they publish posts that resonate with their values. Their tone is natural, so it helps them connect better with their audiences.

When you leverage social media for business, make sure that your posts aren't too pushy or promotional. Instead, create informative and engaging stories so that they resonate better with your audiences.

Social media is a space where your audiences can directly get in touch with you. Encourage them to comment on and share your posts on social media.

Be open to their questions and make sure you are responding courteously to all of their comments. Try to respond to them as soon as possible. You need to build a two-way channel so that you can earn the trust of your customers.

You can leverage social media for your business to build an open channel of communication with your audience.

According to a study by Sprout Social, responsiveness on social media prompted consumers to make a purchase. And 83% of consumers said they wanted brands to respond to them on social media. Honesty, helpfulness, and friendliness were found to be traits that boost social media engagement for brands.

Even while tackling negative comments, be polite. Understand that each comment that you make represents your brand's personality. You may keep the tone casual, but always make sure your manners are in place.

If you find out that there was a mistake on your part, you can try offering discounts. Coupons or freebies may work too.

If a consumer does not seem satisfied with your products or services, reach out to them. Tell them that you'd like to connect with them to learn more about your shortcomings.

This shows your consumers that you truly care for them. In the long run, it will help you build brand loyalty as well.

Another great way of leveraging social media for business is to collaborate with relevant social media influencers. Not only can they help to create buzz about your brand but also build your credibility. This in turn, can actually help you get more conversions.

A study by Twitter in 2016 made some interesting revelations. 49% of Twitter users said that they relied on recommendations and reviews by influencers. Nearly 40% users also admitted to making a purchase as a direct result of an influencer's tweets.

So find relevant influencers in your niche and get them to promote you. Ask them to share reviews of your products that include your website links and social media handles.

When Robby Ayala posted a tweet showcasing the salient features of HP laptops, it was retweeted 22,000 times. It was a simple, light-hearted tweet, but it gave HP a lot of mileage.

Influencers are role models to their followers and so they trust their choices completely. If an influencer likes a product, their followers might give it a try as well.

Influencers focus on engagement. They ask questions, respond to comments, and even conduct quizzes and contests sometimes. If they're backing you, you should expect more engagement on your social media account too.

You've may have great content and interesting products to showcase. However, simply posting them on social media isn't always good enough. You need to also make sure it reaches the right audiences and a number of them.

Organic reach has decreased considerably across all social media platforms in the last couple of years. In a survey by Buffer, 55% of marketers said that their Facebook organic reach had declined in one year.

So how do you expect more of your followers to find your content? Paid ads on social media are the way forward. Leveraging social media for your business may require you to shell out some money for paid promotions.

Exchange of information

But throwing some money in, and expecting it to do wonders for you won't work. You need to understand how ads work on social media.

Try to understand your audience demographics and target your ads to specific users. Only then can you expect some good results.

Once you have posted your ad, you will need to constantly keep a tab on how well it is doing. If you see a particular age group or gender not responding well, tweak your strategy. You can always re-target ads for more effective results.

Also, paid ads work differently on different social media platforms. So invest some time to understand them. Facebook, Instagram, and Twitter – all of them have different strengths.

Choosing the right platform depends on what you expect from your advertisement campaigns. But in general, Instagram is the new domain that digital marketers are hailing for its success stories.

In 2017, Gymshark, a fitness apparel company, ran a Black Friday campaign on Instagram. During this period, 40% of their purchases came from Instagram.

Data from Instagram shows that they were able to reach 16.4 million people through targeted ads. That's a lot, isn't it?

Paid ads can do your brand a lot of good if you use them wisely. Be creative, and don't stick to just one format.

Also explore video ads, carousel ads, and Stories ads which are the latest additions to Instagram ads. Make sure you mix it up and see what works best for your brand.

Social media can drive brand awareness as well as sales. All you need to do is post engaging content consistently and promote it well. Social media can also give you insights into your audience's preferences and tastes.

Leveraging social media for your business can be truly beneficial. However, to leverage its full potential, you need to invest some time into planning. If you are playing your cards right, the results will be sweet for sure.

Do you know any other ways of leveraging social media for business? Share your suggestions or experiences in the comments section below. We'd love to hear from you!

www.ingramcontent.com/pod-product-compliance
Lightning Source LLC
Chambersburg PA
CBHW070820220526
45466CB00002B/728